Among My Souvenirs

by
Alan West

AuthorHouse™
1663 Liberty Drive
Bloomington, IN 47403
www.authorhouse.com
Phone: 1-800-839-8640

First published by AuthorHouse   08/15/2011

ISBN: 978-1-4634-2552-4 (sc)

Library of Congress Control Number: 2011911556

Printed in the United States of America

Any people depicted in stock imagery provided by Thinkstock are models, and such images are being used for illustrative purposes only.
Certain stock imagery © Thinkstock.

This book is printed on acid-free paper.

Forward

A few years ago, I started putting thoughts onto paper in a form of poems. Every thought was inspired by an event that was occurring in my life or an experience I had in early years of childhood. As I've gotten older I tend to remember and reminisce more and more. I was raised in a loving home with hard working parents. They saw to it that we felt safe and secure and received a good education while at the same time enjoying each moment of our daily growth to maturity. We had the very best of holidays, for which you will experience from my poems of Easter, Halloween, Thanksgiving and Christmas. As I got into adulthood I had more thoughts of our existence and of my Christian faith that had been seeded as a child.

I hope you will enjoy these offerings to you as I hope it will bring back the same type of memories that inspired these writings.

Dedication -

In 2005, I went to work as a travel agent. I fulfilled a desire that I had for many years. I retired after 25 years as a police officer. I had also worked as a hotel manager, professional wrestler and a musician. With the experience of these many fields, I felt many ups and just as many downs.

But through these many lessons I learned an important thing. The most satisfying experience is the experience of the heart. This I have learned from 30 plus years with the most wonderful soul mate anyone could ever expect to find. I therefore dedicate these writings of Feelings, Love and Remembrance to the love of my life, Cathy.

Table of Contents

Life's
Everyday

Trials of Life

As I awoke this morning
I soon discovered
That through my trials in life
I have recovered
The dawn arrived and sunshine's rays
Gave light to fact that I've begun new days
Through faults of my own
and those beyond my control
I've moved ahead to make my life unfold
From this day forward I hope to see
A change in my life
A change in me
It took years to realize
But this message I send
I know now, that I'm my own best friend...

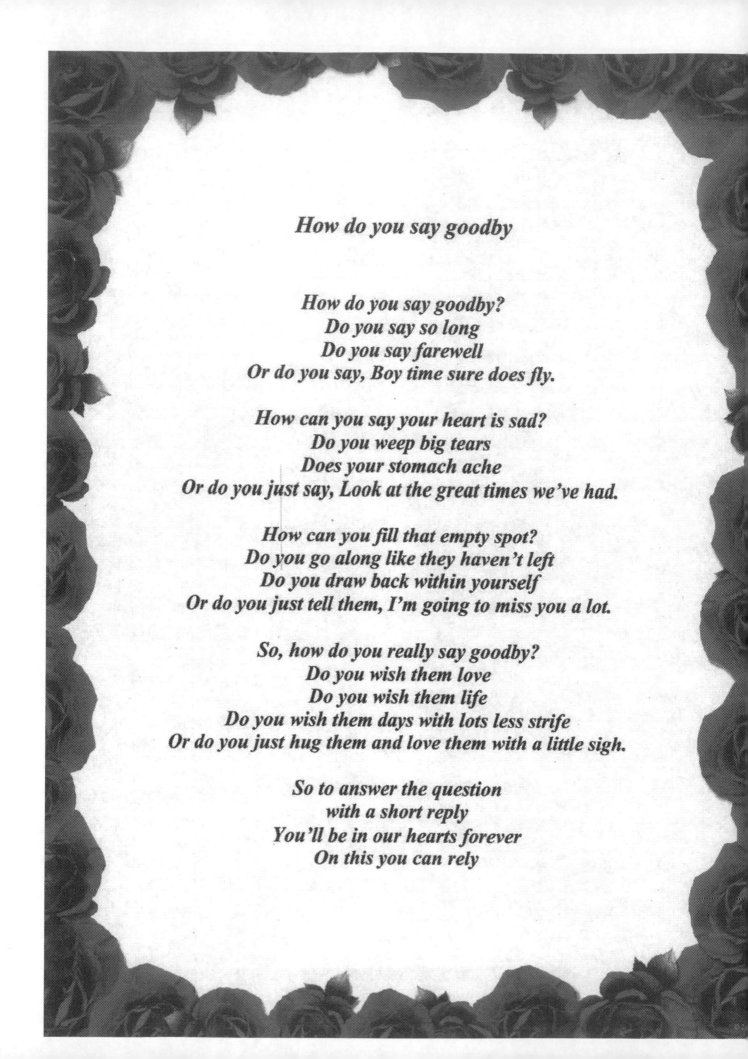

How do you say goodby

How do you say goodby?
Do you say so long
Do you say farewell
Or do you say, Boy time sure does fly.

How can you say your heart is sad?
Do you weep big tears
Does your stomach ache
Or do you just say, Look at the great times we've had.

How can you fill that empty spot?
Do you go along like they haven't left
Do you draw back within yourself
Or do you just tell them, I'm going to miss you a lot.

So, how do you really say goodby?
Do you wish them love
Do you wish them life
Do you wish them days with lots less strife
Or do you just hug them and love them with a little sigh.

So to answer the question
with a short reply
You'll be in our hearts forever
On this you can rely

Life Begins Anew

Next week when I see the sun come up
I'll see a different light
The days that passed around us
have vanished like the night

The love I've felt from all of you
has made my heart grow strong
But the time I'll spend away from you
May make my life grow long

We've shared our lives
We've shared our times
We've laughed and we have cried
And now we see this parting
as ours tears flow and we sigh

But know this from my inner soul
that as a day brings the morning dew
Please don't worry about me
because My Life Begins Anew

The Gift

I ponder the past
I live with the present
and I dream of a future yet to be
The memories of good times
good family and good friends from my childhood
Are vivid for me to see.
But as summer goes to autumn
and winter goes to spring
the days will pass and the years go by
and the present it will bring.
Our memories keep us strong
as each day we live unfolds
The thoughts of how we've lived so far
and how our lives will mould
And then the wind will swirl around
and thoughts begin to soar
and we think, what will the future bring?
What's behind the door?
We dream of a future yet to see
and all fear the unknown
We all know what will be will be
For life is a Gift and not a Loan

Another Chance

I awoke this morning and drew a deep breath
I heard the birds singing as I arose from nights rest
I knew I'd been given another chance to succeed
Another chance at life's follies to turn a good deed

I know I'll be challenged at every bend in the road
But I know that I'll make it no matter how burdened the load
So I'll charge the day forward with God's grace at my back
and conquer my problems and never look back

If you follow my approach with each day as they pass
and turn your eyes forward than to ponder the last
Then you'll find when you lay down tonight as you rest
All your troubles are distant and your life has been blessed

Jean's Poem

Someone that you can count on
when life is going well
But when life turns a dirty face
then they're someone you tell
Someone to compliment you
even when it's not deserved
Someone to stand behind you
When life throws you a curve
These things describe so very few
you'll meet within your time
But if you're as lucky as I have been
You'll find one just like mine
So as we travel our uncertain path
We'll not know what's round the bend
But the one thing we can count on
Will always be our friend

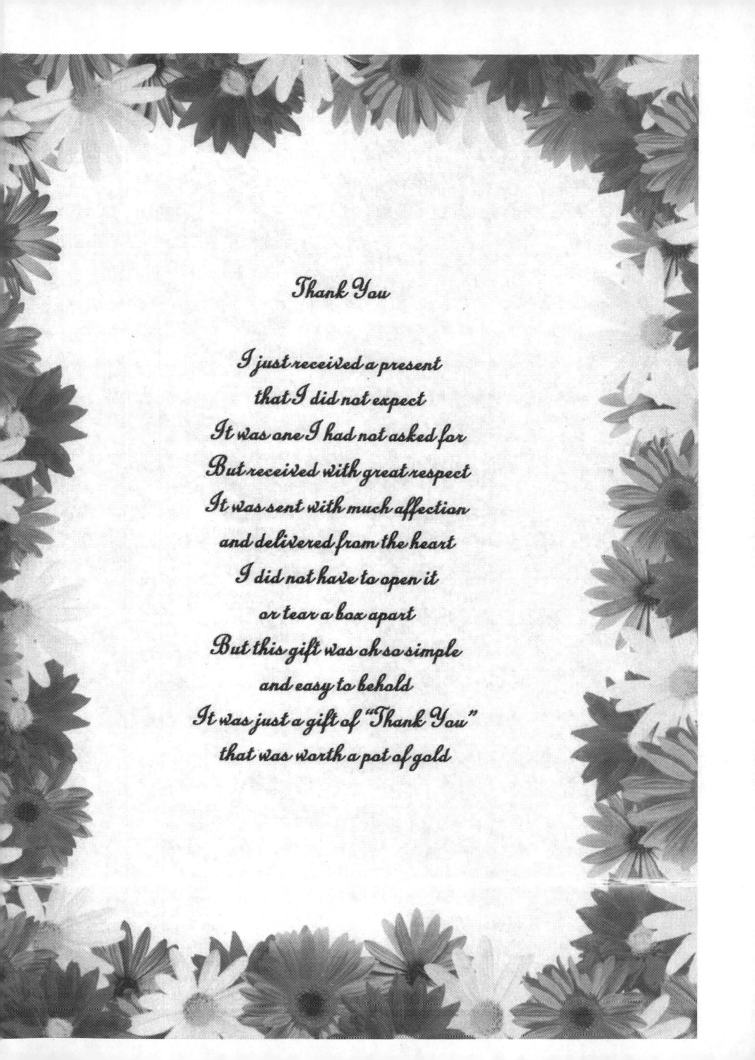

Thank You

I just received a present
that I did not expect
It was one I had not asked for
But received with great respect
It was sent with much affection
and delivered from the heart
I did not have to open it
or tear a box apart
But this gift was oh so simple
and easy to behold
It was just a gift of "Thank You"
that was worth a pot of gold

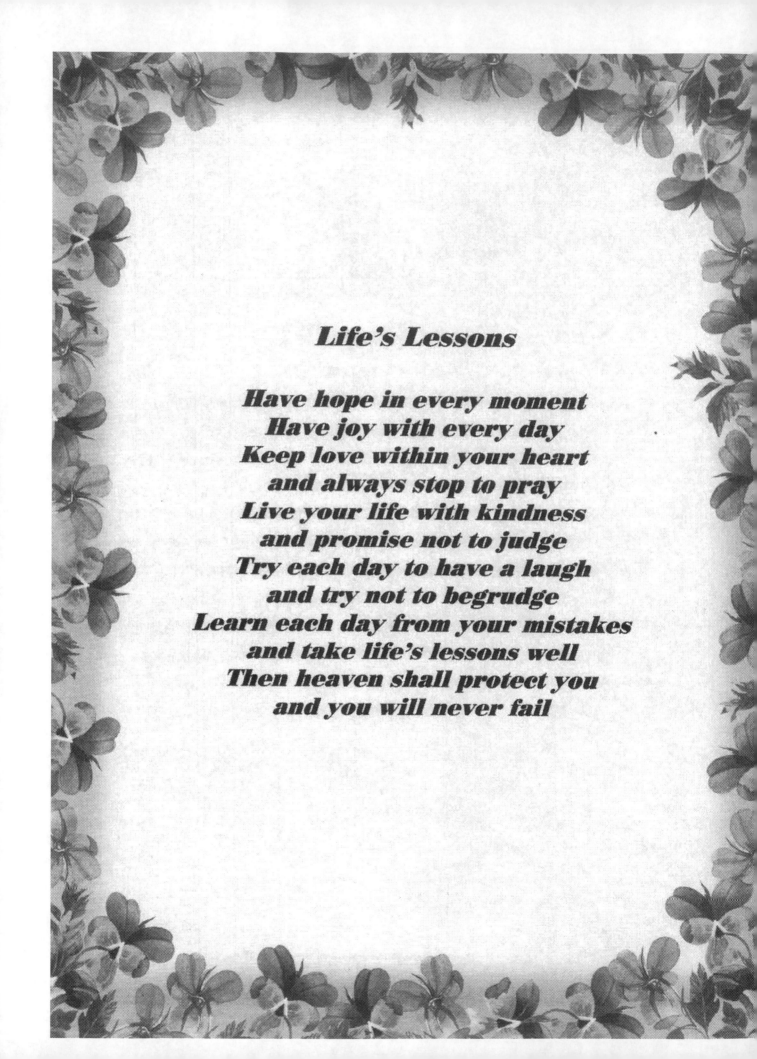

Life's Lessons

Have hope in every moment
Have joy with every day
Keep love within your heart
and always stop to pray
Live your life with kindness
and promise not to judge
Try each day to have a laugh
and try not to begrudge
Learn each day from your mistakes
and take life's lessons well
Then heaven shall protect you
and you will never fail

Where Has All The Time Gone

Every day leads to another day
as weeks lead to months lead to years
But we do not learn how precious time is
until a rock in the road appears
We hurry through life without giving a thought
That time is not on our side
When we should look back at how hard we have fought
as our future we need to decide
God gives us our strength to slowly move on
and ability to think each day through
So we'll never ask, Where has all the time gone?
and we'll capture each moment anew

Life's
Inspirations

The Answer

He'll make a pearl from a grain of sand
He'll catch your tears with his loving hands
He'll make fierce rivers from the mountains flow
He'll give you reasons for your faith to grow

He'll make birds sing as the dawn draws near
He'll fill your heart so you'll loose your fear
He'll be beside you as each day you walk
He'll guide you, He'll teach you
The words that Jesus taught

But as time goes by
and life's days grow dim
He knows that your thoughts
will turn to him

He'll see all that you have learned
He'll give you the knowledge
for which you've yearned

Then you'll see your life
as it grew from that small grain
and you'll know that your troubles
were never in vain

Then as you enter your new home in the sky
He'll finally answer the question, Why?

Reflections

So delicate are our daily lives
More fragile than we know
We should handle it with careful hands
And take it oh so slow
We should measure it with full respect
and plan each step we take
We should stop at times just to reflect
Each morning when we wake
We do not know how far we'll go
Or how we will arrive
We do not know the steps we'll take
Or how hard we will strive
We only know that if we're strong
and faithful to the task
Our lives will be both full and long
Until the very last

The Lesson

Today I felt upon my face

a drop of rain that fell

I closed my eyes for heaven's grace

and prayed that all was well

I asked that good be in our heart

although our task is hard

I asked that we be guided straight

and keep our faith unmarred

Then as I stood there eyes clutched tight

I could hear the songs of doves

and I knew the clouds were replaced with light

by sunbeams from above

The lesson that I learned from this

was that the answer was always here

Just look up with your heart when the skies turn gray

and He'll cleanse you with a tear

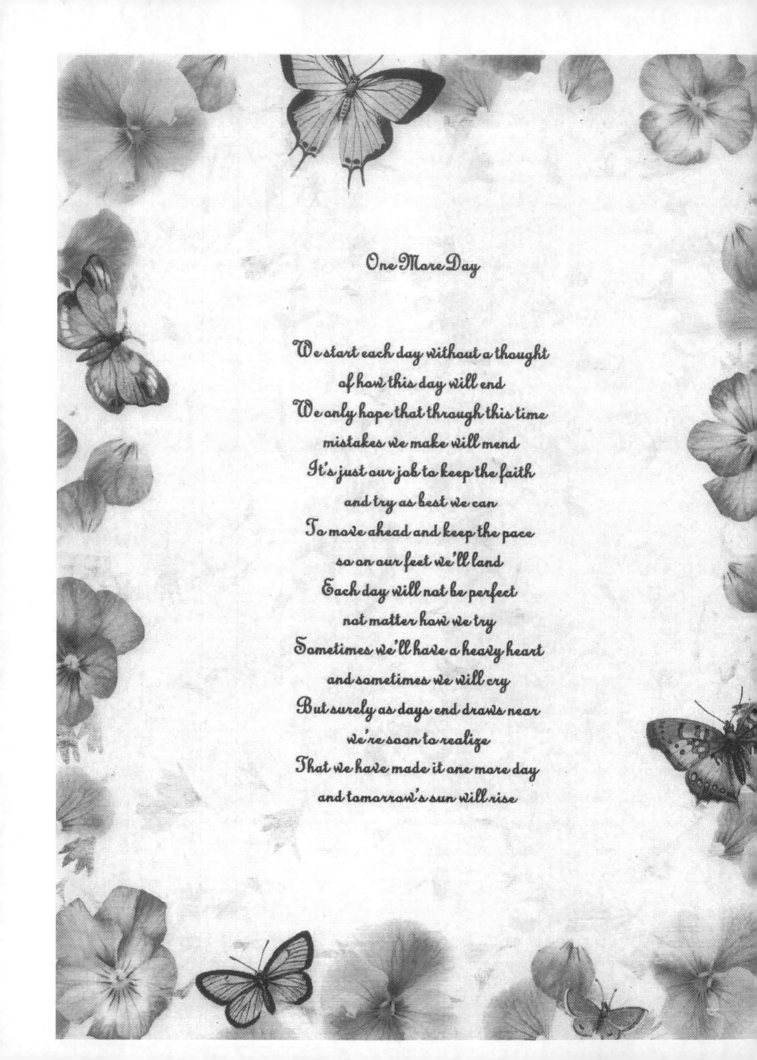

One More Day

We start each day without a thought
of how this day will end
We only hope that through this time
mistakes we make will mend
It's just our job to keep the faith
and try as best we can
To move ahead and keep the pace
so on our feet we'll land
Each day will not be perfect
not matter how we try
Sometimes we'll have a heavy heart
and sometimes we will cry
But surely as days end draws near
we're soon to realize
That we have made it one more day
and tomorrow's sun will rise

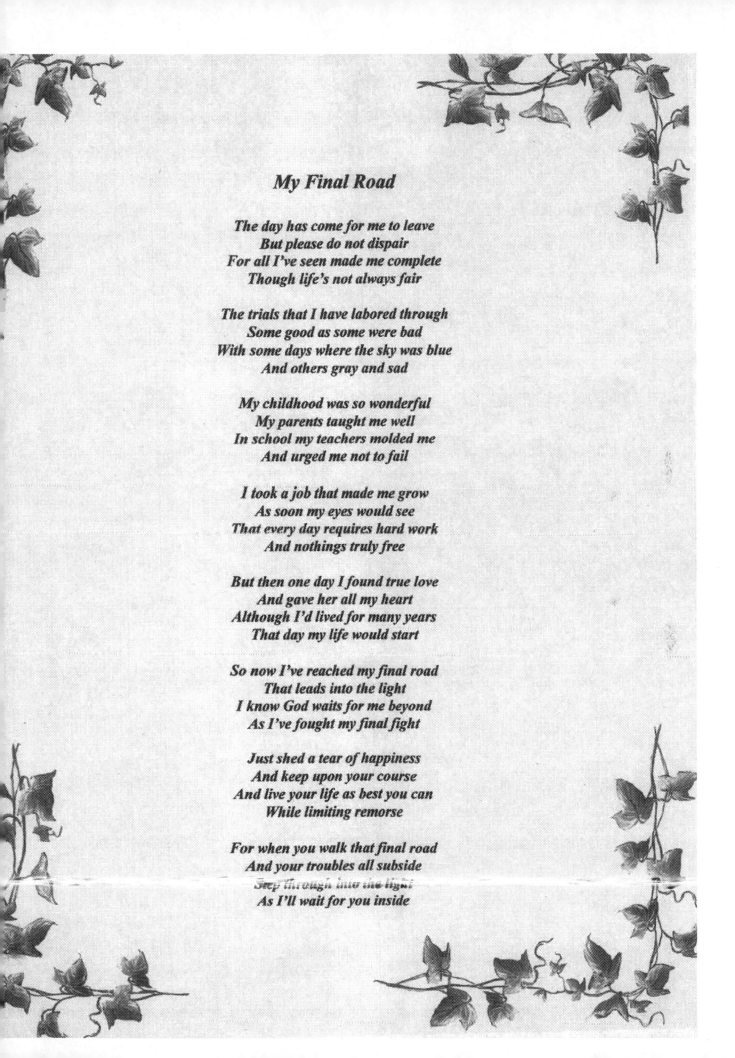

My Final Road

The day has come for me to leave
But please do not dispair
For all I've seen made me complete
Though life's not always fair

The trials that I have labored through
Some good as some were bad
With some days where the sky was blue
And others gray and sad

My childhood was so wonderful
My parents taught me well
In school my teachers molded me
And urged me not to fail

I took a job that made me grow
As soon my eyes would see
That every day requires hard work
And nothings truly free

But then one day I found true love
And gave her all my heart
Although I'd lived for many years
That day my life would start

So now I've reached my final road
That leads into the light
I know God waits for me beyond
As I've fought my final fight

Just shed a tear of happiness
And keep upon your course
And live your life as best you can
While limiting remorse

For when you walk that final road
And your troubles all subside
Step through into the light
As I'll wait for you inside

This Trouble Too Will Pass

The clouds formed above us
and the rain began to fall
The news that we were getting
was devastation to us all
To think this was delivered
to God's greatest fan
However we must realize
that God has got a plan
Never were we promised
that life would bring no pain
But by keeping faith and praying
Our sufferings' not in vain
So close your eyes and give your thanks
for every breath you take
Then walk through life with baby steps
and live for heaven's sake
Each burden that you bear
will be better than the last
For God gives us this promise
that this trouble too will pass

The Lighthouse

As we gaze upon the sea

we stare in awesome wonder

Then ask the question, What's God's Plan

A thought we often ponder

Do we compare the ocean swells

to our daily ups and downs

Do we fight the fight

or give up and run our ship aground

Then we look upon the hill

and we see a lighthouse stand

as we watch the beam of light go out

To lead the ships to land

Then through these acts that we have seen

We understand much more

That if we walk within God's light

We'll surely reach his shore

A Touch from God's Own Hand

Today I looked around and thought
I am so ashamed
For all complaining I have done
I'm the one to blame
I see so many people
that battle through each day
working hard to get ahead
and juggling who to pay
Our lives are complicated
and filled with endless stress
So we must hold our heads up high
and God will do the rest
We must rise above our woes
and by each other stand
Then on our backs we'll feel a pat
A Touch from God's Own Hand

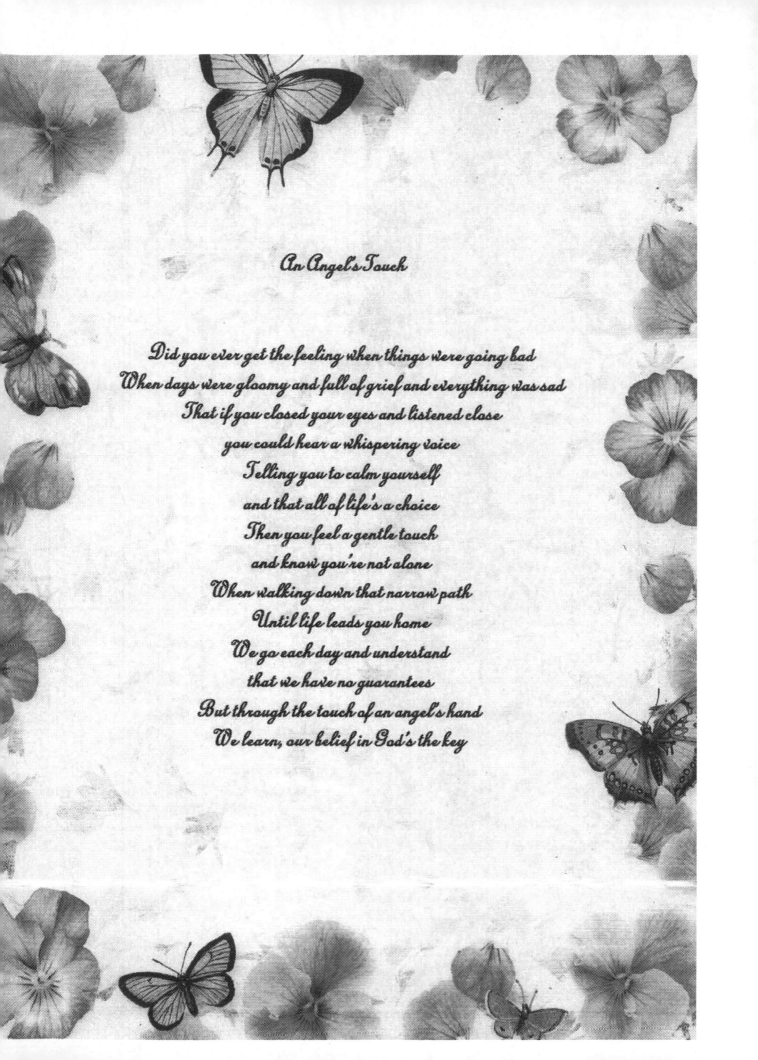

An Angel's Touch

Did you ever get the feeling when things were going bad
When days were gloomy and full of grief and everything was sad
That if you closed your eyes and listened close
you could hear a whispering voice
Telling you to calm yourself
and that all of life's a choice
Then you feel a gentle touch
and know you're not alone
When walking down that narrow path
Until life leads you home
We go each day and understand
that we have no guarantees
But through the touch of an angel's hand
We learn, our belief in God's the key

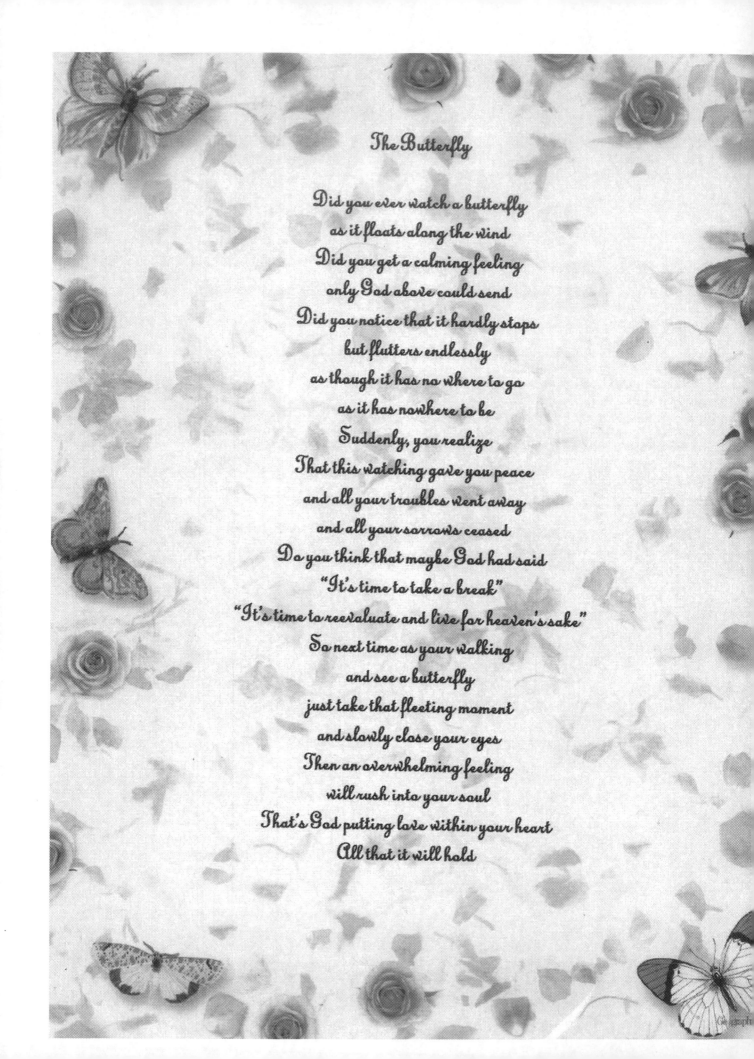

The Butterfly

Did you ever watch a butterfly
as it floats along the wind
Did you get a calming feeling
only God above could send
Did you notice that it hardly stops
but flutters endlessly
as though it has no where to go
as it has nowhere to be
Suddenly, you realize
That this watching gave you peace
and all your troubles went away
and all your sorrows ceased
Do you think that maybe God had said
"It's time to take a break"
"It's time to reevaluate and live for heaven's sake"
So next time as your walking
and see a butterfly
just take that fleeting moment
and slowly close your eyes
Then an overwhelming feeling
will rush into your soul
That's God putting love within your heart
All that it will hold

The Road to Glory

Every step we make and turn we take
leads us down the road to glory
As we move on down that winding path
each mile tells a new story
Sometimes our choice will lead us wrong
then we must stop and pray
That God will make us look ahead
as he will point the way
We might slow down to a crawl
and we may get stuck in mud
But by our faith we'll move along
as God's promise is understood
Then as we reach that final hill
we'll climb with all our might
As we reach out and take his hand
and walk into God's light

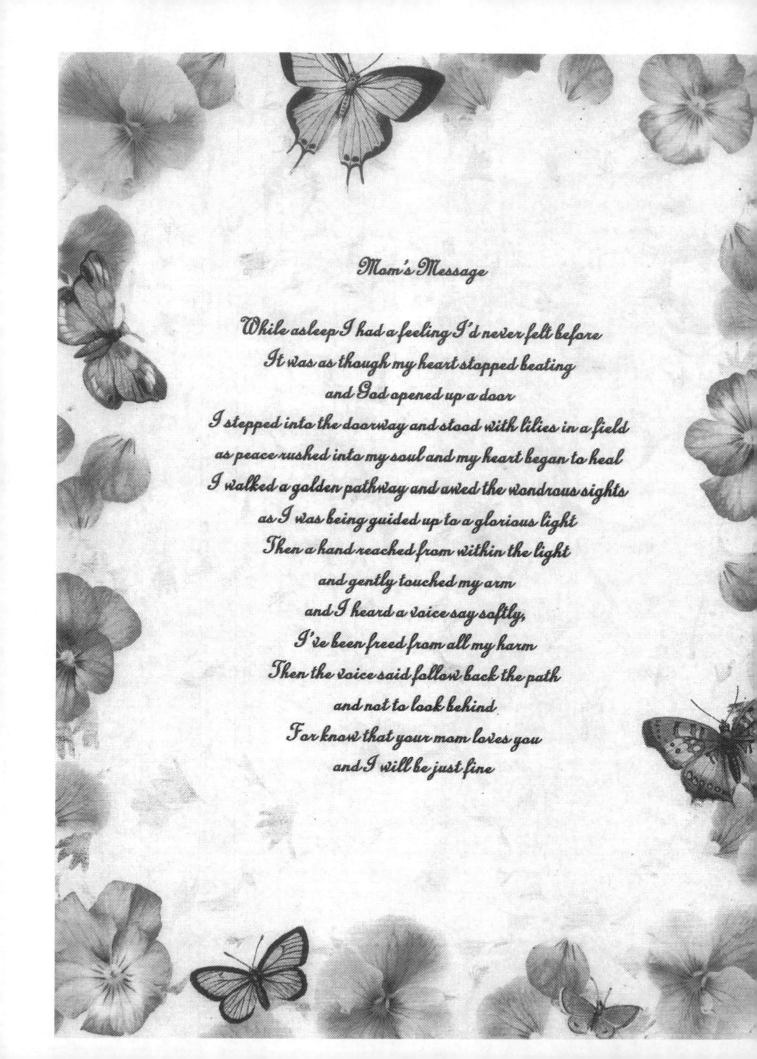

Mom's Message

While asleep I had a feeling I'd never felt before
It was as though my heart stopped beating
and God opened up a door
I stepped into the doorway and stood with lilies in a field
as peace rushed into my soul and my heart began to heal
I walked a golden pathway and awed the wondrous sights
as I was being guided up to a glorious light
Then a hand reached from within the light
and gently touched my arm
and I heard a voice say softly,
I've been freed from all my harm
Then the voice said follow back the path
and not to look behind
For know that your mom loves you
and I will be just fine

The Dream

I looked across the mountains
with it's early morning smoke
and I said, God has blessed this place
as no truer words were spoke
I saw the snow atop the peaks
as eagles soared about
I felt the air upon my face
This was heaven's breath, no doubt
I could smell the winter foliage
and hear the brisk cold streams
I was sure that this was God's own place
A place derived from dreams
Then I awoke and realized
from this dream's very start
That God was building heaven
Deep within my heart

How Beautiful Heaven Must Be

When we approach our next great task
All the wonders we will see
When pain and sorrow and troubles have past
How beautiful heaven must be
When angels sing sweet songs to our soul
And our worries of life are set free
With our hearts filled with joy and our days in control
How beautiful heaven must be
We'll walk wonderful gardens by each stepping stone
And stroll by the great endless sea
We'll talk to our savior as he sits by the throne
How beautiful heaven must be

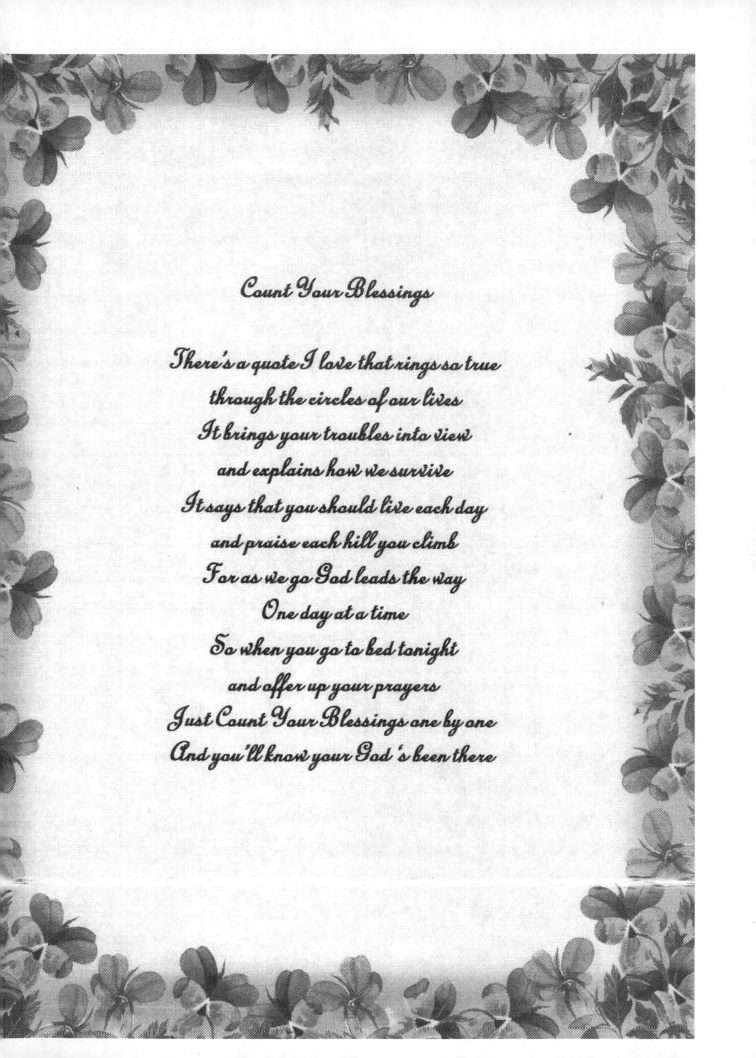

Count Your Blessings

There's a quote I love that rings so true
through the circles of our lives
It brings your troubles into view
and explains how we survive
It says that you should live each day
and praise each hill you climb
For as we go God leads the way
One day at a time
So when you go to bed tonight
and offer up your prayers
Just Count Your Blessings one by one
And you'll know your God's been there

Who We Are

Did you ever wish that you could change
the person that you are
Did you think if you were someone else
that you'd be better off by far
Would you have rather been a CEO
or some star on TV
Should you have taken a different branch
on your great family tree
God has laid our road ahead
and only he knows where we'll go
So he has chosen what we'll be
what part of God's great show
We just need to trust in him
and give thanks for what we do
Then we can walk each day with pride
Knowing our job's important too

Precious Memories

I keep my precious memories
deep within my mind
As I grow old I'll always know
these memories I can find
Some days when I'm a little sad
I can think of Christmas past
With all the fun that day we had
building memories that would last
I'll remember back to my first car
and how I drove around with pride
I'll remember my days with mom and dad
and how I felt the day they died
I hold my memories ever close
as each day they help me grow
Until the day I close my eyes
and Jesus says, "Let Go"

Heaven's Bay

As we sail through our daily lives
we encounter many storms
Each horizon that we see
will take on many forms
Some days no wind will fill our sails
and we'll slow down to a crawl
Then many times strong winds prevail
and find us in a squall
But we've been given a great promise
that the skies will turn bright blue
And though we face so many storms
our faith will lead us through
So sail away along the waves
and feel the ocean's spray
For God will send his angels
to guide us home to heaven's bay

Life's Happiness

We embark upon a winding path
from the day of our first breath
We'll travel through each bend and curve
till this road will end in death
But each day as we walk on this great path
We develop as we go
Learning all along the way
life refining as we grow
But Gods' placed the greatest burden
within our own two hands
To decide just who we want to be
and how we'll lay life's plan
For although God is our architect
with each blueprint he'll assign
the job to find life's happiness
For this is our design

Can You Imagine

Can you imagine mornings when the sun would never rise
Can you imagine silence when a baby never cries
Can you picture how the world would be
without friends to help you bear
Could you live your daily lives
if you had nothing but dispair
So keep the faith and read His word
each day as it begins
For God sent his son into this world
to shoulder all our sins
Use wisdom as you move ahead
Don't treat life as a whim
For can you only imagine
What life would be without Him

The Lottery of Life

We buy a lotto ticket
and our thoughts begin to soar
If our number hits tonight
our work is nevermore
We'll buy a stately mansion
and travel endlessly
We'll see great sights we've never seen
and go on a shopping spree
But if that number does not draw
Don't think that you've been passed
For your lotto ticket to heaven
will not be unsurpassed
You'll move into God's mansion
as your travels lead you home
You'll see great sights you've never seen
and you'll never need to roam
Our life upon this earth is tough
and the lotto is a dream
But if you follow the master's rules
You'll gain your God's esteem

How Much Do You Think You Are Worth

Is your worth from your checkbook balance
Are you judged by the cloths that you wear
Do your words earn respect
Does your lifestyle reflect
that you're considered by all to be fair
For many years past this decision was made
and your value was paid on a cross
His unquenchable thirst to bear all our sins
He succumbed to the ultimate loss
So He walked on this land from the day of his birth
and gave of himself to all
Till the day that he paid what He thought you were worth
As he answered His Father's call

Rainbows

I looked toward the sky
as the rain came to an end
and saw a thing of beauty
only God himself could send
A bright array of colors
arched across the clear blue sky
A rainbow sent from heaven
to pass the storm on by
From this God teaches patience
for He'll drive dark clouds away
with a promise of salvation
and a love He'll not betray
So do not be discouraged
when the skies of life turn dark
For God will place a rainbow
deep inside your heart

Life's Rising Tide

It seems so never ending
all the days of hurts and bumps
When our spirits fill deflated
and our lives are in a slump
Then we reach a low when we can't see
what's beyond the coming hill
as we think our life has lost control
and we've truly lost our will
That's when our heart starts growing
Getting bigger from within
God's filling it with goodness
and purging us of sin
He promises us each day we walk
He's ever by our side
He'll lead us to His summit
To avoid life's rising tide

We Hope We'll Make You Proud

Mom and Dad would always say
they should have taught us better
But not a day will pass us by
their wisdom we won't mutter
As children they would dry our eyes
and make us to sit straight
while teaching us to bow our heads
and pray that God is Great
As we grow old each thing we do
will mirror all they've taught
For everything that we have learned
could never have been bought
So Mom and Dad while looking down
We hope we'll make you proud
We'll remember everything you said

Live Life to the Fullest

Everyday is seems to me
We find time to complain
The weather's bad
The coffee's cold
To all things we disdain
But what we do not realize
Is that God has laid our course
These things are planned so we may learn
How to conquer and go forth
Life's not meant to be an easy road
Each day new things we face
It's how we handle every turn
And problems we embrace
So let not your heart be troubled
As these daily problems pass
Just live life to the fullest
As each day may be the last

** I recently received an email that my nephew serving with the Air Force in Afghanistan sent home. From this email I wrote "You Will Win the Day" and dedicate it to Christopher Davis and all of his Comrades serving a grateful nation around the globe. . .

You Will Win the Day

Today I joined a long sad line
As I stood among my friends
To watch my comrades going home
As their war had met it's end
I felt a tear roll down my face
As reality set in
And gazed up to the heavens
And said "This one we must win !"
History has taught us
And the Bible tells us so
That we must battle every day
As Evil is our foe
Some days we must lift the sword
And charge the Devil's hand
While other days are turned about
And we must make a stand
So whatever we must face
And whatever comes our way
Keep God within your heart
And You Will Win the Day

Tunnel of Life

My heart was so troubled
And my days had no end
How will I get through this?
Will my heart ever mend?

The skies just turned darker
As I just could not see
Why the God that I loved
Had done this to me

Then as I moved onward
From this day filled with strife
I realized God led me
Into a tunnel of life

The deeper I went
The darker it turned
I prayed ever stronger
As God's wisdom I yearned

Then I heard a voice say
"If in me you abide"
"You'll emerge from this tunnel
To new light outside"

God knows that our troubles
Can cause us to doubt
He knows that we wonder
What life's all about

He just asks that we trust him
And keep our faith strong
For the song says, We'll know more
Farther Along

The Messengers

Each night I lay me down to sleep
As I think back on the day
I vision angels guiding me
In all I do and say

I hold a hand that I can't see
That guides me on a path
Avoiding problems facing me
Avoiding trouble's wrath

I do not question where I'm led
I just follow as I must
For I know it's God that leads me on
And in Him I must trust

These messengers surround us every day
And watch our every move
They listen to us when we pray
While our trust in God we prove

So in your prayers before you sleep
Just add another line
And thank the angels watching you
As they follow God's design

Trust in the Angels

I fall to my knees
And pray to heaven above
Take all hate from my heart
And replace it with love

For life is too short
To dwell on the past
Just capture each moment
And pray that it lasts

Keep walking forward
When troubles abound
And trust in the angels
That God sends around

Soon you'll feel your life changing
And new horizons you'll see
As the hate leaves your heart
And your spirit's set free

Seasons Change

Today I heard a bluebird
As he began to sing
I saw a tulip blooming
And knew that it was spring

I saw everything around me
Awaken from winters nap
As Gods creations came to life
As if theyd been unwrapped

The beauty of this dawning day
Gave truth to His own word
That through the bible we are taught
His promise is assured

He promises the seasons change
As long as this old earth remains
And all our lives will cycle through
Just as all the seasons do

But dont forget what God has said
The greatest promise of them all
That someday heavens voice will speak
And youll hear heavens call

Through faith youll hear a voice come through
A voice youll never doubt
Saying whosoever comes to me
Will never be cast out

Ref — Genesis 8:22 and John 6:37

Life's
Special Days

MARDI GRAS
WELCOME JUNE 14 81 ABOARD

Mardi Gras

Our Wedding Day

I arose this morning and began a new life
A day long awaited and planned
The memories of childhood have all cycled through
The hourglass of sand

Today I must change much that I do
And reconsider the decisions I make
For new responsibilities I bear
And all are not for my sake

But with all I will change and all I will do
Never have I felt so much joy
For the love this day I feel in my heart
Is a feeling I can hardly employ

In a few hours I will stand before God
And make promises to one I adore
And pledge to her my unending love
That will last beyond God's great shore

Now it's time to move forward and say to my love
That I love you in every way
I give to you the gift of my heart
On this Our Wedding Day

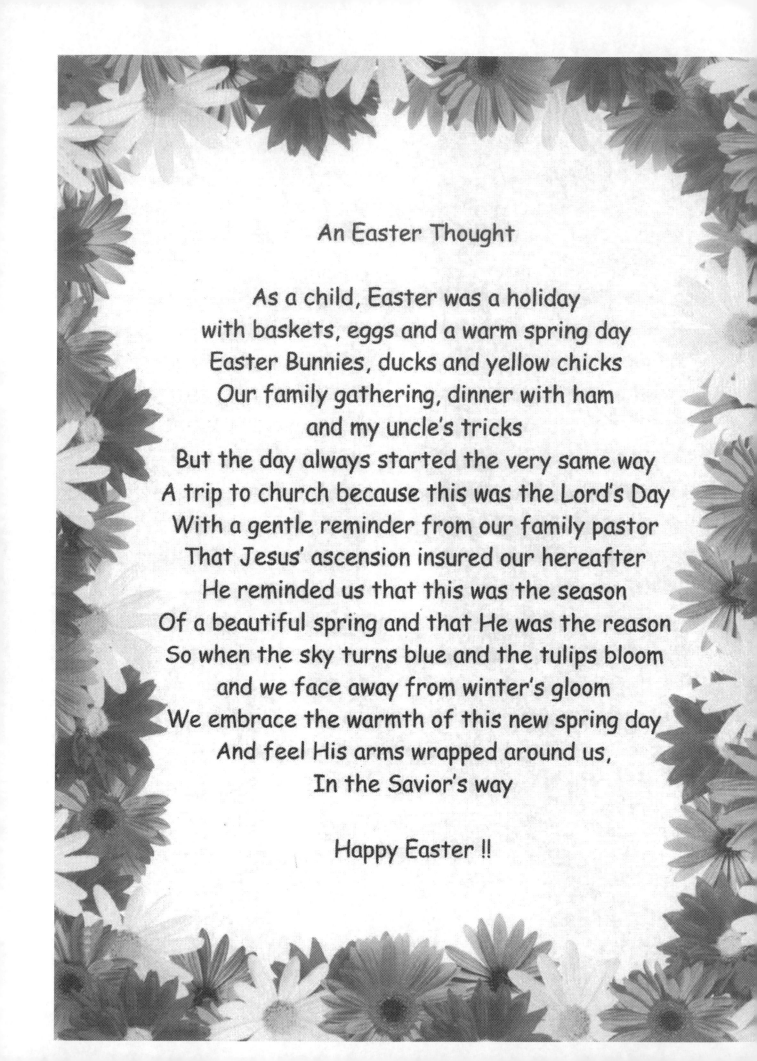

An Easter Thought

As a child, Easter was a holiday
with baskets, eggs and a warm spring day
Easter Bunnies, ducks and yellow chicks
Our family gathering, dinner with ham
and my uncle's tricks
But the day always started the very same way
A trip to church because this was the Lord's Day
With a gentle reminder from our family pastor
That Jesus' ascension insured our hereafter
He reminded us that this was the season
Of a beautiful spring and that He was the reason
So when the sky turns blue and the tulips bloom
and we face away from winter's gloom
We embrace the warmth of this new spring day
And feel His arms wrapped around us,
In the Savior's way

Happy Easter !!

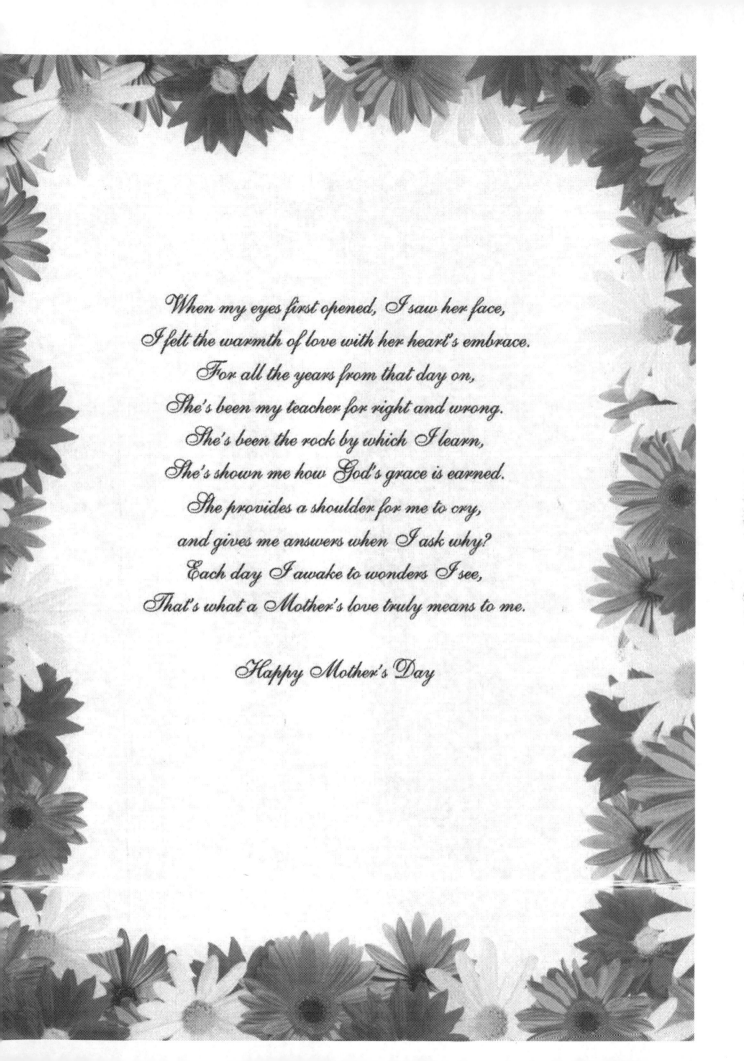

When my eyes first opened, I saw her face,

I felt the warmth of love with her heart's embrace.

For all the years from that day on,

She's been my teacher for right and wrong.

She's been the rock by which I learn,

She's shown me how God's grace is earned.

She provides a shoulder for me to cry,

and gives me answers when I ask why?

Each day I awake to wonders I see,

That's what a Mother's love truly means to me.

Happy Mother's Day

A Mother's Love

Once a year we celebrate
A love that's pure and plain
a feeling of devotion
that cannot be explained
A breath of life that fills our lives
each day and evermore
A comfort that fulfills our days
As we've never felt before
We know that in the days that pass
sometimes we'll stumble and we'll fall
But then support comes ever fast
and brings us back up tall
Through timeless ages years go by
But this will never alter
On a Mother's love you can rely
This love will never falter.

Happy Mother's Day

God's New Show

Summer draws a final breath
as leaves begin to color
The squirls are gathering hickory nuts
and playing with each other
Steamy days and sultry nights
are cooling with the season
The curtain rises on God's new show
and changing landscapes begin to flow
and this is done for us to know
His love's the lasting reason

Life's Journey

The days are getting shorter
and the nights are turning cold
and we're painted a picture of yellows and gold
The wind starts to swirl and whistle a song
as it signals the hot days of summer are gone
The harvest brings pumpkins and apples for pie
bringing smells from the kitchen of days gone by
Moms' cooking chicken and baking the bread
From this bounty of goodness God's creatures are fed
The wonders are many when falls' season arrives
as we see daily changes in all of our lives
Just as sure as the season brings beauty to bare
We'll travel life's journey and rely on our prayer

Halloween Night

The night air cools and the leaves are all falling
with the harvest moon bright Halloween comes a-calling
We dress in odd costumes and jack-o-lanterns we light
then we go door to door on this spooky fall night
We see ghosts and goblins and scarecrows and such
as we yell "trick or treat" filling bags that we clutch
Popcorn balls, apples and candy of all kinds
can't wait to get home, on this bounty we'll dine
We watch movies of monsters like wolfman and mummy
while eating our treats and filling our tummy
I can't wait till next year when we do this again
We will gather more pumpkins and feel the fall wind
We'll all get dressed up and more lanterns we'll light
with all of the fun next Halloween Night

Halloween Had Come Again

As a child this day was lots of fun
and came but once a year
When the moon was bright on this crisp fall night
and creepy sounds you'd hear
It's said this night that zombies walk
and come back from the grave
That bats will fly and ghosts will talk
as your parents say, "Be Brave"
Then we'd walk around from house to house
not knowing what we'd meet
Would we get an awful fright!
Or would we get a treat
Then home we'd go with bags of loot
and stories we could tell
While listening to the hoot-owl hoot
that made your skin turn pale
We'd start to sing the Monster Mash
and dance around the room
Cause Halloween had come again
and we hope is comes back soon

Thanksgiving Day

We always start this day the same
with Macy's big parade
Mom has got the turkey in
and the pies are being made
We thrill as we watch the bands march by
and awe at the balloons
We squirm in anticipation
because Santa's coming soon
Then that jolly man goes down the street
and the parade comes to an end
Now football comes on TV
and Dad is in the den
Mom makes the announcement
that dinner time is here
and the family gathers roundabout
and bow our heads in prayer
"Thank you Lord for the food we eat"
"and in our hearts you'll stay"
"May peace abound with joy around"
"as we have a Happy Thanksgiving Day"

Christmas Cheer

Oh! The brisk cold falling snow
blankets the ground to start winter's show
The mercury falls and we bundle tight
as we sing Christmas carols and candles we light
Singing Joy to the World and O Little Town
as our friends and family all gather round
We'll share pumpkin cake and Christmas punch
as we tell stories and laugh over holiday lunch
We'll all watch the kids with all their new toys
and think back to when we were girls and boys
We recall those days when surrounded with love
as we turn our eyes upwards and thank up above
Then we'll say our goodbys
from this day we've held dear
and dream a repeat
of this day for next year
Now we all know the meaning of real
"Christmas Cheer"

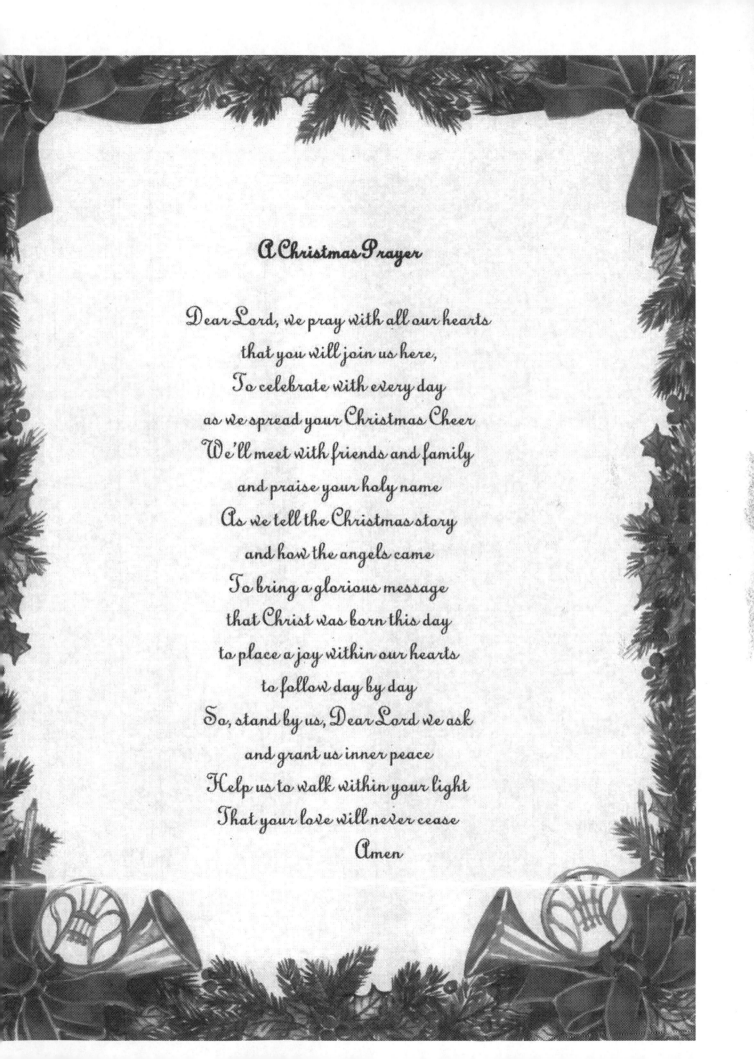

A Christmas Prayer

Dear Lord, we pray with all our hearts
that you will join us here,
To celebrate with every day
as we spread your Christmas Cheer
We'll meet with friends and family
and praise your holy name
As we tell the Christmas story
and how the angels came
To bring a glorious message
that Christ was born this day
to place a joy within our hearts
to follow day by day
So, stand by us, Dear Lord we ask
and grant us inner peace
Help us to walk within your light
That your love will never cease
Amen

Santa's Coming

Santa's coming, time to go to bed

Twas the Night Before Christmas

has already been read

The presents are wrapped the tree has been trimmed

candy canes hang from each delicate limb

The fire is roaring and the stockings are hung

The radio's playing as carols are sung

Mom's still baking and the smell's in the air

Cakes and cookies she's making with her own loving care

Then we stare at the star atop of the tree

and we think, is this what the wise men did see ?

Did this lead them to the place where the Christ child was born

In the crisp cool air of the first Christmas morn

Did they kneel in the presence of this wonderful sight

And know they'd been guided by a heavenly light

Then we knew, what they knew from this miracle birth

the true meaning of the saying, Peace on Earth

Then off to our beds and on our knees to pray

Thanking God for his love and for Christmas Day

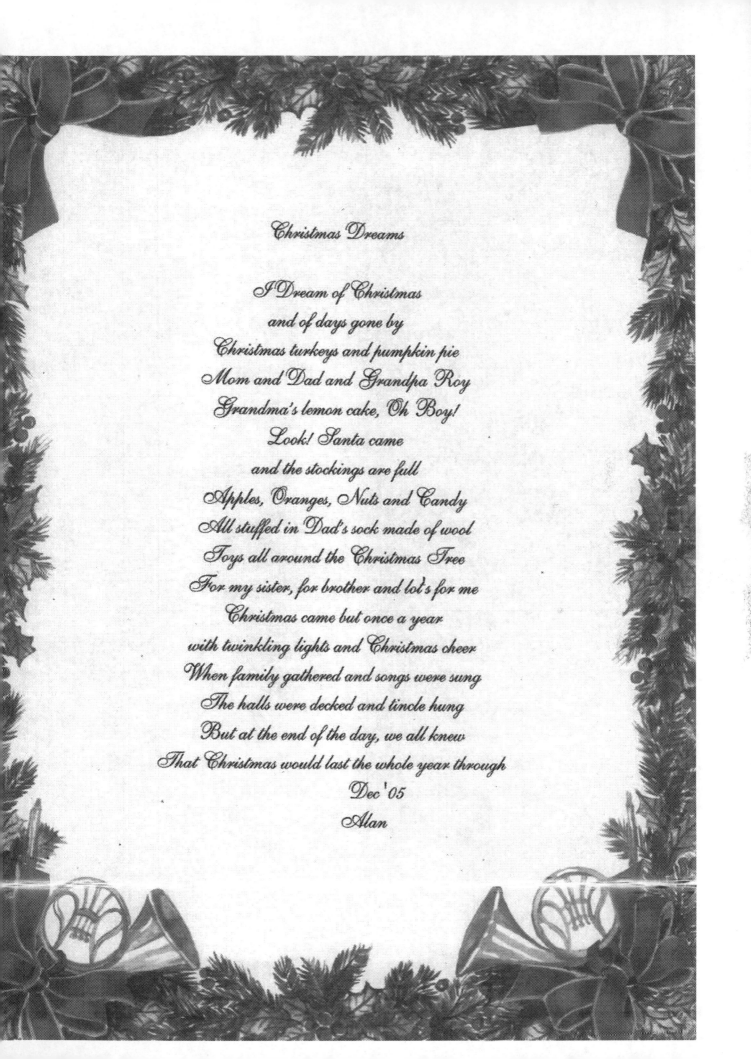

Christmas Dreams

I Dream of Christmas
and of days gone by
Christmas turkeys and pumpkin pie
Mom and Dad and Grandpa Roy
Grandma's lemon cake, Oh Boy!
Look! Santa came
and the stockings are full
Apples, Oranges, Nuts and Candy
All stuffed in Dad's sock made of wool
Toys all around the Christmas Tree
For my sister, for brother and lot's for me
Christmas came but once a year
with twinkling lights and Christmas cheer
When family gathered and songs were sung
The halls were decked and tincle hung
But at the end of the day, we all knew
That Christmas would last the whole year through

Dec '05
Alan

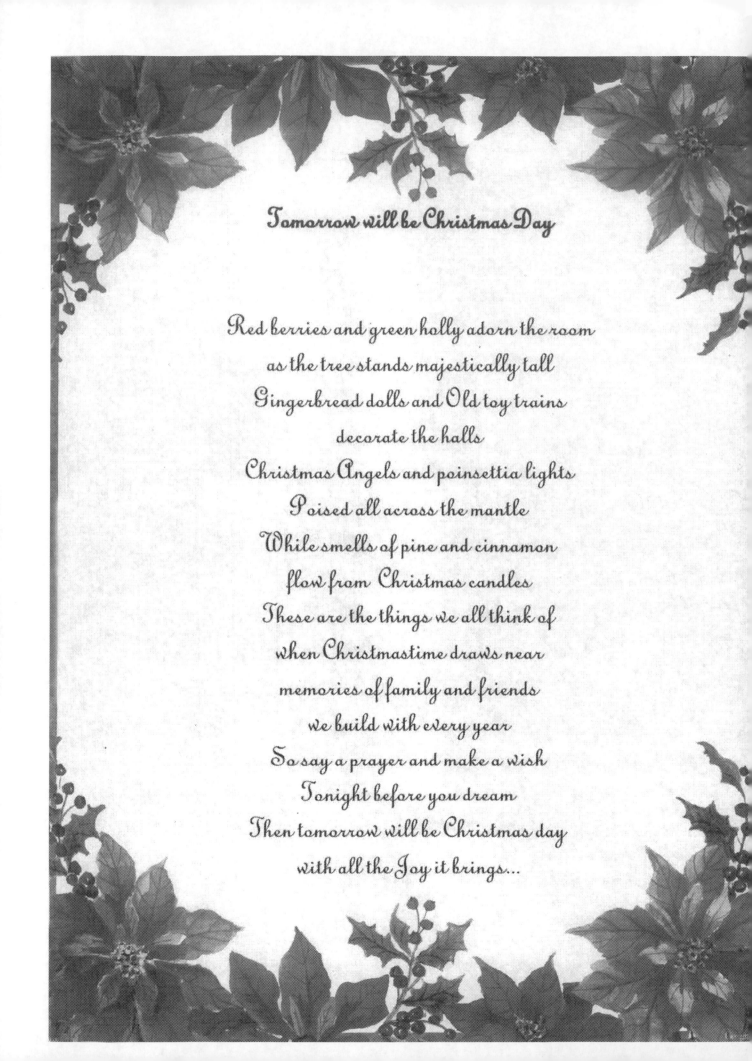

Tomorrow will be Christmas Day

Red berries and green holly adorn the room
as the tree stands majestically tall
Gingerbread dolls and Old toy trains
decorate the halls
Christmas Angels and poinsettia lights
Poised all across the mantle
While smells of pine and cinnamon
flow from Christmas candles
These are the things we all think of
when Christmastime draws near
memories of family and friends
we build with every year
So say a prayer and make a wish
Tonight before you dream
Then tomorrow will be Christmas day
with all the Joy it brings...

God Bless Us Everyone

Christmas trees and holly leaves
and wreaths of evergreen
Carolers singing with holiday cheer
while the snowfall sets the scene
Cinnamon fragrance fills the air
from pies and apple cider
Mom and Dad are wrapping gifts
while our eyes are getting wider
As we watch from the window and stare at the sky
just to see if reindeer really do fly
Then the radio says, "Santa is coming"
and off to our beds we all go running
We'll close our eyes quickly and drift off to sleep
But if not, we'll just lay there
and not make a peep
Then before we know it Christmas day will arrive
and under the tree into presents we'll dive
Merry Christmas Mom ! Merry Christmas Dad !
To each we will say
Santa was sure good to us on this wonderful day
Then later that day when the turkey is done
I'll say to us all
"God Bless Us Everyone"

Lone Bright Star

A lone bright star shown high above
amidst the eastern sky
To announce the birth of purest love
a gift from our Most High
From that night on our lives would change
as everyone would learn
For this is what God had arranged
His purest love we'd yearn
God said, "I'll send a little child to spread about my word"
"That my love is both pure and strong but it must be deserved"
So this child became a teacher to roam across the land
and spread his message from within
to every grain of sand
Now every year on a winter night
we'll see this lone bright star
and we'll know that this is God's own light
Love's message from afar

Christmas Eve

I lay in bed one Christmas Eve
as excitement filled my mind
Thinking about where Santa was
and what he'd leave behind
Sis always got a Barbie doll and lots of girlie stuff
and brother got an army suit he thought made him look tuff
I got tanks and army men and lots of other toys
But I knew our day was better
than many girls and boys
So as I said my prayers that night
I thanked God up above
For all the Christmas' we've had
that filled our house with love
So Santa if your running short
and don't have enough on hand
Put our names on the bottom of your list
We will understand

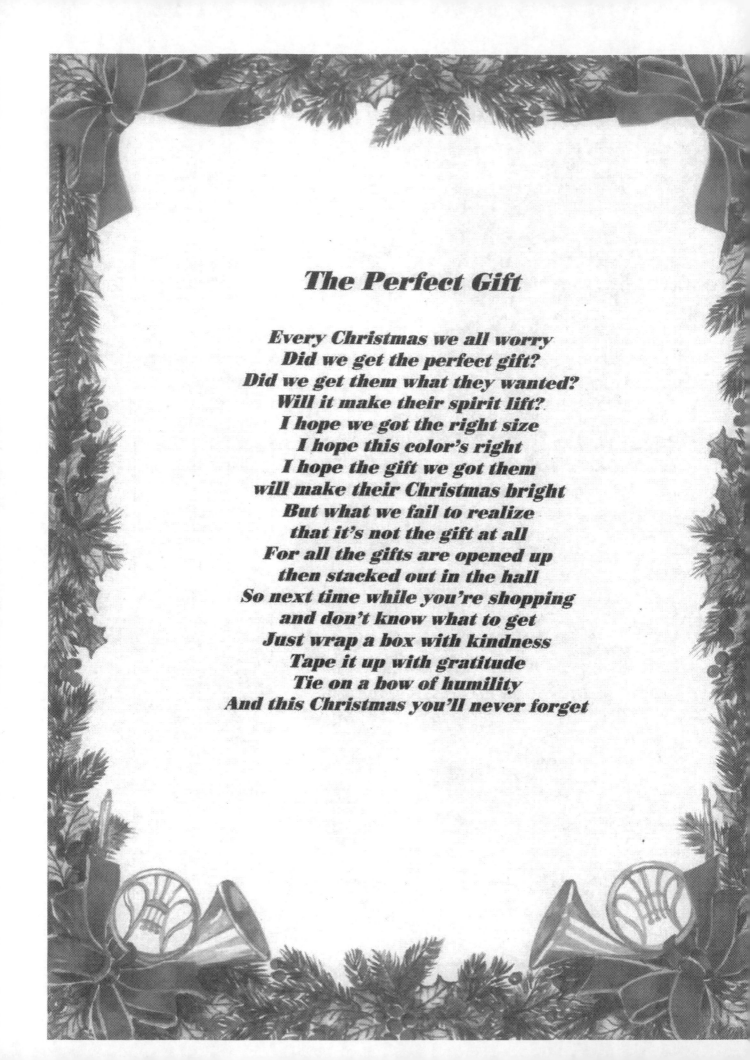

The Perfect Gift

Every Christmas we all worry
Did we get the perfect gift?
Did we get them what they wanted?
Will it make their spirit lift?
I hope we got the right size
I hope this color's right
I hope the gift we got them
will make their Christmas bright
But what we fail to realize
that it's not the gift at all
For all the gifts are opened up
then stacked out in the hall
So next time while you're shopping
and don't know what to get
Just wrap a box with kindness
Tape it up with gratitude
Tie on a bow of humility
And this Christmas you'll never forget

The Most Important Gift

Many years ago
on a dark crisp winter night
God sent a gift of peace and joy
to fill this world with light
He wrapped this gift so lightly
and in a manger lay
Then shown a star upon this place
to glorify this day
Many years have come and gone
and we still celebrate this birth
For this gift of love and hope
was the most important gift on earth

Christmas Everyday

Decorations round the room
And outside sleigh bells ring
Christmastime is here again
Just hear the angels sing

Going shopping endlessly
To buy for those we love
While walking through the crowded stores
With twinkling lights above

Tonight we'll have a party
And all our friends will come
We'll eat and sing and toast our glass
And tell jokes that are dumb

Why should we just feel this joy
One time of the year
Why not keep this love alive
Each day with Christmas cheer

New Year's Resolutions

Each time the New Year rolls around
we make our resolutions
Will we not smoke, will we lose weight
Will our finance find solutions
But more than not the promise fades
and we find we've not improved
For with each day these thoughts evade
and desire is then removed
So set your goals and set them high
and get yourself on track
For we need to remember
It's ourselves that hold us back